Meeting special needs

A practical guide to support children with Autistic Spectrum Disorders

by Collette Drifte

In memory of Kiernan and Spencer Frampton,
both very special people with
their own special needs.

In this book the use of he, him or his is gender neutral and is
intended to include both sexes.

Step
forward
PUBLISHING

Published by Step Forward Publishing Limited
St Jude's Church, Dulwich Road, Herne Hill, London, SE24 0PB Tel. 020 7738 5454
© Step Forward Publishing Limited 2007 www.practicalpreschool.com

Meeting special needs. A practical guide to support children with Autistic Spectrum Disorders ISBN: 978-1-904-575-15-3

Contents

- Introduction   4

- What exactly are autistic spectrum disorders?   5

- How can an autistic spectrum disorder be recognised?   7

- How can the setting support the child?   10

- How can I help the child manage his behaviour?   13

- How can the setting support the child's carers?   15

- How does the setting work with other professionals?   19

- The inclusive SEN Policy   20

- Useful Contacts   24

Pages to copy and use:

- Example of an Individual Education Plan (IEP)   Inside Front Cover
  for children with Autistic Spectrum Disorders

Introduction

If you are looking at this book, it is probably a safe bet that you have a child in your setting, or are about to admit a child into your setting, who has an autistic spectrum disorder (ASD), or autism. As more children diagnosed with the condition are placed within a mainstream setting, then clearly more practitioners are going to be working with them. It is a sad fact that there is no compulsory element or module for learning about ASDs in trainee educational professionals' courses, and over 70% of schools are not satisfied with their available in-service training in the subject *(National Autistic Society website, accessed 18th May 2007).*

Practitioners often want to know how to identify an ASD, what to do to support the child, how they can work with the child's carers and how they themselves can be supported. Perhaps you too would like to have these questions addressed. Whatever your reason for picking up this book, I hope that within it you will find answers to some of your questions about ASDs, and ideas for things you can actually do to support the child in managing his condition within your setting.

This book is a starting point and it gives you background information and lots of practical suggestions for action you can take.

Remember you are not on your own. Your setting should have an inclusive special educational needs (SEN) policy in place, and a designated Special Educational Needs Coordinator (SENCO) who should work closely with you to help the child achieve his potential. While it is not the job of the SENCO to work on a one-to-one basis with the child (unless, of course, he happens to also be the child's key practitioner), he is there to offer you support and advice. Even if he doesn't know the answers to your questions himself, he will know where to go for those answers.

There are also organisations such as The National Autistic Society, the Autism Research Unit, and parent support groups that will help you. You will find contact details of these and other supporting organisations at the end of the book. Take the opportunity to get in touch and listen to their advice and suggestions.

Scattered through the book are case studies which serve as examples to illustrate a point being made. They are all studies of real children, but their names have been changed. You will also come across a Pause for Thought section every so often, where an issue will be introduced which gives you an opportunity to ponder practice a little more deeply, and possibly to discuss and share with your colleagues.

Before we move on to the main body of the book, allow me to say a few words about terminology. I still hear people referring to an autistic child, or, less positive, an autistic or, even worse, an aut. It behoves us as professionals to relentlessly pursue and model the correct approach, ie. that the child is a child first and foremost, who happens to have a condition or disability known as ASD. So you will find this book refers to a child with autism or a child with autistic traits.

What exactly are autistic spectrum disorders (ASDs)?

Most practitioners know the terms autism and autistic spectrum disorders and are more aware of children with autism, or indeed are these days more involved with them. But if you ask a practitioner what exactly an autistic spectrum disorder is, he may find it hard to give a detailed answer, although he may be able to list some of the 'typical' traits.

Within the wider population, there is still a lot of fear and misunderstanding about the condition and also, sadly, a lot of prejudice. In this section, we will look at the wide range of ASDs and see how we have reached the point where we are today.

The condition was once called autism, and it was used to refer to people who had severe communication and social disabilities. Over the last twenty-five years or so, however, professionals working and researching in the field have realised that there are many people who have some of the characteristics of autism, but who are not as severely affected as others. This wide range (spectrum) of abilities led to the term autistic spectrum disorders or ASDs. The condition known as Asperger's syndrome (pronounced with a hard 'g' as in 'garden') is also on the autistic spectrum, and you may sometimes see the term autism/Asperger's spectrum, to show that the full range of ability is in the same category.

How long have we known about ASDs?

It is possible there have always been people with autism, but it was not until the late 1930s that the condition was recognised. Here is a whistle-stop history of developments:

1938: Leo Kanner, an Austrian child psychiatrist based in the USA, began to study children with similar 'autistic' behaviours.
1943: Kanner published his research, using the term early childhood autism.
1944: Hans Asperger, a Viennese paediatrician, identified a group of children with normal or above-average intelligence but with difficulties in communication and social interaction (hence Asperger's syndrome).
1979: Lorna Wing and Judith Gould began to study children in Camberwell, London. They found that there were some with other symptoms who could also be described as having autistic traits.
1988: Lorna Wing coined the term autistic continuum to include the larger number of children identified with similarities to Kanner's group, but not quite fitting his description.
1996: Lorna Wing went on to use the term autistic spectrum, to allow for a broader definition of autism.

From the 1990s to the present time there have been huge advances in the research and identification of the condition, and in ways of supporting people who have it.

How many children have an ASD?

The numbers have dramatically risen in Britain, the USA and other western countries since about 1979. The increase in incidence and diagnosis could be because practitioners and carers know more about the condition and can recognise it more easily these days.

- most studies suggest there are between four and six children in every 10,000 with the autism that Kanner identified.

- the National Autistic Society suggests that one child in 100 is affected, if you include the widest spectrum (website accessed 18 May 2007).

- all studies show boys outnumbering girls, with figures ranging from 5:1 (Lord and Schopler, 1987) up to 2:1 (Ciadella and Mamelle, 1989). Most studies show an average of four boys to one girl, but when a girl has autism, she is usually quite severely affected.

What causes ASDs?

Unfortunately, we still don't have a definitive answer to this question. Research is going on all the time and you can keep up to date with developments and findings by getting in touch with the National Autistic Society or the Autism Research Unit (at the rear of this booklet).

Over the years, though, some definite information about autism has been discovered. Here's some of it.

- There is probably a genetic element involved. If one identical twin has autism, there is about a 60% chance the other has it too. But they may not have it to the same degree – one might be very disabled while the other is very able.

- The brain activity and brain circuits of a person with autism are different from those of somebody not affected.

- In some people with autism, an important chemical in the brain known as serotonin is produced in higher quantities. This higher level has also been found in close relatives even when they are not affected themselves.

- Some children may have a problem with their immune and/or chemical system that leads to autism. Researchers suggest that viral infections, mercury poisoning, gluten and casein allergy or yeast problems may be among the causes. These theories have yet to be proved.

- The hair and blood samples of children with autism show a much higher level of environmental poisons than samples from children without autism. Among these poisons are aluminium, lead and antimony, a flame-retardant chemical in household products.

It seems that taking all these findings together, it is likely that an ASD can occur in a child with a certain genetic makeup, and/or who is affected by environmental toxins which affect his internal systems and his brain.

Fears, wrong ideas and mistakes about autism

There are all sorts of ideas in circulation about people with an ASD, which have come to be accepted as true. Many of these have been disproved through research but, sadly, some people still believe them, so let's do a bit of myth-exploding.

- You can't cure an ASD. This is true in the sense that there aren't any pills, treatments or medicines that somebody can take to 'get better' from autism. But because we understand more about the condition and how to manage it, there are children with an ASD who have learnt to overcome the traits that prevented them from leading full and successful lives.

- People with autism have an outstanding gift of some kind. This idea is commonly accepted because of films and television programmes about some people with autism who do actually have a great talent. It is true that there are children with an ASD who have an outstanding gift, often with numbers or mathematical-based skills such as music or technical drawing. Their talent is usually in a single area and they are often poor at most of the other skills and abilities needed to manage their everyday living. But the majority of children with an ASD don't have an extraordinary talent.

- People with an ASD can't form relationships or show emotion. This is another popular idea that is not necessarily true. There are children who have an ASD and who show their feelings in a 'normal' way, but we are not aware of their disability because we don't see them as 'different'. It is true that some children with an ASD don't seem to make relationships with the people around them, but we can't say that it is the case with all of them.

- People with autism have severe mental disabilities. This is no more true of people with ASDs than of the whole population. Among children with an ASD there is a wide range of abilities, from very able to severely disabled. If you don't include children with Asperger's syndrome, then about 75% of children with an ASD have a learning difficulty of some kind. Some children are very sensitive to their environment or find it hard to make their bodies do what they want. This may give the impression that they have learning disabilities.

- A person with an ASD is a genius. Again, this is not any more true of people with an ASD than of the population as a whole. There are claims that some of the cleverest people in history probably had autism, for example, Einstein, Beethoven, Thomas Jefferson and Isaac Newton. While there might be something in this, we have got to remember that for every Beethoven there are hundreds of thousands of ordinary people getting on with their ordinary lives.

- Anybody with some of the symptoms of autism has an ASD. Again, this is a wrong but popular belief. Almost all of us has one or two of the characteristics of an ASD, but we don't all have autism.

How can an autistic spectrum disorder be recognised?

There are not any tests *per se* that can diagnose an ASD. It is the way a child behaves that gives clues to practitioners, because children with an ASD do certain things that are nearly always the same. A diagnosis of autism before the age of two is rare, so signs and symptoms during babyhood are often gleaned from carers' memories.

Before we talk about what you need to look for, it is important to remember that if a child does show any of the following signs or symptoms, you must not jump to the conclusion that he has an ASD. Only a doctor can tell that, but you will have a description of the child and his development that will help the doctor in making a diagnosis. Be sure, too, to share your observations with the child's carers.

You also need to bear in mind that no two children are the same. It does not follow that all children will experience all the problems, nor to the same degree of severity. Each child is unique and will have his own set of symptoms, but the following section gives some of the general and common difficulties that children with autism experience.

Children with an ASD have problems in three areas known as the Triad of Impairments described by Lorna Wing. Let's have a look at this triad.

- ***Impairments of social interaction.*** This means how the child makes relationships, or not, as the case may be. There are four main types:
1. The aloof child, who behaves as if other people don't exist;
2. The passive child, who is not totally cut off from other people but will not start conversations or activities;
3. The 'active but odd' child, who will speak to other people and become involved with them, but in a very one-sided way, always talking about himself and his own interests;
4. The over-formal, stilted child, who shows this behaviour in later adolescence and who is excessively polite and correct in the way he behaves towards other people.

- ***Impairments of communication.*** This means the child has problems with the way he communicates with other people. His actual grammar and vocabulary may be fine (although not always) but it is the way he uses language that causes the difficulties. There are four main problems:
1. Using speech, where the child's speech development may be delayed and atypical, with repetitions of words, phrases and questions or even staying silent;
2. Understanding speech, which can range from not understanding anything to having some quite good understanding;
3. Intonation and voice control, where the child may have problems controlling the loudness of his voice (either too loud or too quiet), or the 'naturalness' of its tone, where he can sound like a robot;
4. Using and understanding non-verbal communication, where the child has problems using and understanding gestures, facial expressions and body language.

- ***Impairments of imagination.*** This means the child does not develop imaginative play and make-believe games like other children do. This is why a child with an ASD has difficulties in understanding other people's emotions and sharing ideas. Because he does not get pleasure from imaginative play, he falls back on his special interests for enjoyment. (This is why these children often have rituals or repetitive activities.)

What should I be looking for?

Let's look at some things that children with an ASD will do. Decide whether these describe the child about whom you have a concern.

As a *baby* he may:

- start to develop normally at first but then slow up or even go back;
- have feeding problems, often being unable to suck;
- either be happy to lie in his pram all day without crying, or
- scream uncontrollably all day;
- find nappy-changing, dressing or washing unpleasant;
- not reach out for a cuddle or to be picked up;
- not lean out of his pram to look at things, or point them out to his carers;
- be fascinated by things he sees such as bright lights, spinning objects, or things that shine or twinkle;
- be fascinated with music;
- not join in baby games such as Peek-a-boo or Pat-a-cake;
- be delayed in his physical development, not sitting up, crawling, walking at the usual stages;
- not babble or coo.

As a child he may have problems with each area of the Triad of Impairments which can show up in these ways:

With *Impairments of Social Interaction* the child may

- use an adult to get what he wants, but without asking. For example, by taking the adult's hand and putting it on the required object;
- pull away if you try to touch him, avoid cuddles or walk past you without seeming to see you;
- enjoy rough and tumble play, often laughing aloud, but then becoming aloof when the game's over;
- be detached from other people, showing no sympathy if they are hurt or upset;
- avoid looking people in the eye or have problems holding eye-contact;
- find it hard to mix with other children or to copy them;
- be unable to share books, games or conversations with other children;
- hold or hug other people too tightly without realising it is seen as 'odd' behaviour;
- become aggressive if you do not give him the attention he wants.

With *Impairments of communication* the child may

- have delayed or atypical speech;
- repeat the words spoken by other people, especially the last word or the last few words (this is called echolalia), often copying an accent and way of speaking;
- use the same phrase or ask the same question over and over again;
- have problems using 'linking' words such as in, on, under, because, sometimes leaving them out altogether, for example, 'Go bus school';
- confuse opposite words such as off and on or up and down;
- confuse words in pairs such as shoes and socks or brush and comb;
- find it hard to understand when to use the words I and you, often confusing them;
- have normal speech but sound old-fashioned and 'odd' in the words he uses;
- talk non-stop about his favourite subject or interests;
- have difficulty with words that sound the same but have different meanings, for example, meat and meet or saw and sore;
- think words or phrases mean exactly what they say, for example, if you say 'I laughed my head off at a joke', the child will think your head fell off;
- has problems understanding jokes or puns and word play;
- use a 'special' voice (ie. not his own) when speaking to somebody;
- have a mechanical voice so he sounds like a robot;
- find it hard to understand facial expressions, gestures and body language.

With *Impairments of imagination* the child may

- have problems with imaginative play, even with toys that help with imaginative games;
- play with toys in a repetitive or odd way, for example, continually lining them up in the same way or spinning them;
- avoid joining in with other children's imaginative activities;
- enact a character from a book or a television programme, usually repeating the action over and over in the same way;
- enjoy videos and television, especially cartoons, science fiction or films with lots of action and flashing lights, and quiz or 'reality' shows with lots of clapping and noise;
- like stories on tape because they never change, or if you read them a story it has to be in exactly the same way every time.

Here are some other things you might recognise in the child.

- certain noises and/or light may cause unusual reactions. The child might be distressed by, fascinated with or completely unaware of a specific sound (for example, a motorbike) or type of light (for example, camera flash). The child could ignore

one sound, be terrified of another and be fascinated by yet another;
- sensations through bodily touch can cause unusual reactions. Smell, touch, taste, temperature and/or vibration can distress the child, fascinate him or be totally ignored by him. Many children are completely unaware of pain and will not come for comfort when you think they have hurt themselves;
- the child may refuse to eat anything except a very small variety of foods; some children eat very little. It is thought the children do not realise they are hungry. They might also drink excessive amounts of water, juice or tea, sometimes to the point of being sick;

- he may have a ritual that he repeats over and over again; for example, insisting that the tins in the cupboard are always put in the same place, displaying his possessions in a specific way that never changes, always taking the same route to the shops;
- he may have unusual behaviour such as hand-flapping, head-rolling, rocking from front foot to back while he is standing, jumping up and down, finger-flicking, twisting his face around, walking on tiptoes with a springy step, and so on. If you try to stop him doing these things, he can become extremely upset.

Make sure you keep meticulous records – this is very important

Even anecdotal evidence is useful since, often, specific examples of bizarre speech or behaviour can provide important clues as to the difficulty the child has and how to address it. For instance, 'cocktail party' conversation can mislead a busy professional into thinking the child's language is fine, particularly if his speech is clear and his syntax is perfect. But if the same social phrases are repeated day after day and no deeper or relevant conversation is forthcoming, it is time to be alerted.

Check whether the child's hearing is sound *(no pun intended!)*

Clearly hearing and speech and language are linked, and if there is an undetected hearing problem, it is vital this is identified as early as possible. It is vital you establish at what level the child is operating in all aspects of his language development.

Assess both the child's receptive and expressive language skills if you can

If anything in this section rings a bell with you, it is crucial that you get help for the child. Identifying a problem early will save a lot of problems later on, as well as making sure the child develops the vital skills he needs to help him achieve his potential.

Pause for thought

Think of one child you have worked with in the past, who puzzled you, perhaps because some of his behavioural traits were similar to those we have just looked at.

Take a few minutes to write down your thoughts. When you have read all this book, come back to this question again, and have another ponder in the light of your new knowledge.

What was it about the child that made you wonder how he ticked? Did you share your thoughts with anybody in the setting? Did you speak to the child's carers about your feelings? How did you work with the child in the end? Looking back, do you feel your planning for the child was appropriate? Did it help the child to achieve and develop? If the answer is Yes, could or would you have done anything more and/or differently? If No, what would you change about the approach you took?

How can the setting support the child?

It goes without saying that you and the child's carers need to form a good and supportive relationship. By helping each other, you will all be helping the child. Your everyday dealings with the child should be positive and encouraging, without criticism or judgement if some skills have not yet developed fully. Any learning or behavioural difficulties that the child has because of his ASD need to be supported in the setting.

Under the current legislation, ASDs are classed as special educational needs (SEN), and therefore you must plan appropriate support for the child, work with his carers and other involved professionals, work with the child when possible, and keep his carers informed of everything you want to do.

It is very important that you understand how the ASD affects the child, because you can then plan appropriate work and treat the child with consideration and support. For example,

- is the child's ASD alongside another difficulty, for example, emotional and behavioural problems, speech and language problems and so on?
- is the child comfortable with being touched?
- is there anything specific that upsets the child, such as a colour, a noise or a change in routine?
- do you need to give instructions one bit at a time?
- does the child need to have things repeated two or three times before he fully understands?
- does the child find it difficult to work in a particular way, for example in a group of other children, or on his own either with an adult or another child?

It is crucial to know about things like this so you can plan the day's activities to include the child, and to ensure he is happy and comfortable with what you are asking him to do.

How can I involve the child?

Where possible, try to make sure that the child knows what is going on when you start to work with him and his carers. Even young children can be involved at a level that suits their understanding. If you and the child are able to communicate, here are a few tips:

- speak to the child about his difficulties and why he needs support. Explain that you want to help him develop his skills because you love him;
- explain that you are all planning an Individual education plan or Play plan together to help him make progress. Being part of the team becomes very real and very important to him;
- make sure he understands the targets of his IEP or Play plan, if possible and appropriate. If he sees what it is all about, he will be happier at being involved and he will be keen;
- watch for any signs of stress and anxiety, and talk calmly and positively to the child. Encourage him to share his fears with you;
- if other professionals are involved, make sure the child is not scared about them or of them. Explain that they have been specially trained to help children with the same type of difficulties;
- make sure the child knows he can always go to his key worker when he wants to, and also to any other adult in the setting he wishes;

Clearly, not all children with an ASD will be able to communicate at this level, but use your knowledge of the child, and your discretion to pitch your discussions with him at just the right level for his involvement and understanding.

What about Play plans or IEPs?

If you are working in a pre-school setting, working with the child's carers to develop a Play plan may offer a framework for a positive home/setting project. Play plans are great for supporting the child at home and to reinforce and practise what he is doing in the setting.

You and the carers should decide
- which skill(s) you are going to work on (maximum of three);
- how you are going to help the child develop the skill(s);
- what games and activities you will use;
- what rewards you will give the child when he reaches his target(s);
- how often you will use the Play plan and write what happened;
- when you will get together again to check the child's progress, (ie. the review).

Here is an example of a Play plan.

Play plan for Dominic Jones and Dominic's family

Dominic will play these games to help develop interactive/cooperative play and to take his turn.

Targets

1. Dominic chooses a toy or game (not the jigsaws) and plays positively with it together with brother Declan for two minutes, then increasing by a minute each time he reaches his target. When Dominic reaches a target, he can play alone with his jigsaws for the same length of time or more if he wants. For this target, give Dominic a maximum of two games to choose from. You can increase the number of games when he is ready for bigger choices. If two minutes are too long for Dominic to play positively with Declan, reduce it to one or even half. Let him have the session with the jigsaw as soon as he reaches his target.

2. Dominic, Declan, Mum and Dad take turns to choose a board game. Dominic takes his turns during the game. Let Dominic keep the record of who chose the game by sticking the smiley faces on the chart next to each person's name, every night. For this target, give free choice of game to whoever has the turn that night. Dominic fills in the record chart. Have fun playing the game, encouraging Dominic to take his turn properly. Stop the game straight away if Dominic refuses to wait his turn and explain why. (Don't let him play with the jigsaws afterwards if this happens.)
If Dominic's tired or fed up during any of the game sessions, finish them quickly on a happy and enjoyable note.

Here is what Dominic did

Monday 13th September. Dominic chose Connect Four and played with Declan for thirty seconds before having a major cob. I stopped the game and he didn't have his jigsaws. We played Happy Families in the evening (Dad's choice – I think he's trying to tell me something!) and Dominic was great for about two minutes.

Tuesday 14th September. Dominic chose Connect Four again. He played well with Declan for one minute and forty seconds. He then played with his jigsaws for about ten minutes. I chose snakes and ladders. Dominic would not wait for his turn so we stopped the game.

Wednesday 15th September. Today was great. Dominic and Declan played with their Lego for about three minutes with no fights. I let him play with his jigsaws till teatime. Dominic chose snakes and ladders and he waited his turn every time. He didn't want the jigsaws (shocks all around!).

Thursday 16th September. Dominic was a bit niggly today and only lasted three minutes with Declan on the Jackstraws. But I let him go with his jigsaws because he got more than his two minutes target. Declan chose Jackstraws again for the family game and Dominic went totally off the wall so I put the game away and he didn't have his jigsaws. I think he was tired.

Friday 17th September. Could not do the programme because we had to take the boys to Auntie's birthday tea.

Saturday 18th September. Dominic was brilliant today. He played with Declan in the garden for about ten minutes, taking turns on the swing and climbing frame. He had ten minutes with his jigsaws. Dad chose Operation and we had a great time. Dominic took his turn and didn't throw a wobbly.

Sunday 19th September. We went to Grandma's and Dominic and Declan played with Grandad's old train set. They were at it for about half an hour and no fights (Bliss.) Dominic didn't want the jigsaws when we got home so we all played Jackstraws. I chose it to see what would happen after Thursday night, but it was great. We played for about ten minutes.

Dominic and Declan usually play their game while I cook the tea. We play the family games in the evening before bedtime. I think it is beginning to sink in with Dominic.

Date when this Play plan was finished at home.

Sunday 19 September, 2007.

Individual Education Plan (IEP)

Older children will usually have an IEP rather than a Play plan. When you plan an IEP (maybe together with the educational psychologist or an Early Years Support practitioner who has specialised in working with children who have autism), you should involve the child's carers and the child if possible. Your knowledge can be pooled with the carers' to make sure that the IEP is effective.

The IEP will include

- which skills are going to be worked on;
- how they are going to be developed;
- who will be working with the child;
- how often the IEP will be used;
- how the child's success will be measured;
- when he should have achieved his targets;
- when the IEP will be reviewed.

It is important that you watch the child's progress in the IEP activities you do in the setting. The IEP can always be changed if it is not helping the child.

When you carry out activities with the child, try to follow these suggestions:

- do the IEP in short bursts of activity to prevent the child from becoming tired and irritable;
- make sure the activities are fun to do and the child continues to enjoy them;
- make sure there is a tangible way of recording progress so the child can see his hard work is paying off;
- give him games and activities specifically geared to his target skill;
- consistency and routine are crucial; if the child knows exactly what is going to happen during a session, he can concentrate on what he is doing without worrying about what comes next.
- explain the game or activity before you start;
- give the child time to practise new skills. He needs to feel confident in what he has learnt before he moves on to the next target. Ask his carers to let him show off his new abilities to the rest of the family.

Here is an example of a completed IEP:

Child's name: *Dominic Jones*   **DOB:** *13.2.2003*
Date IEP implemented: *30.9.07*   **Code of Practice level:** *Early Years Action*

Areas of strength: *Dominic enjoys the jigsaws. He will work on them for up to thirty minutes. He's interested in toy vehicles, particularly trains.*
Areas of concern: *1. Dominic shouts out during group activities.*
    2. Dominic plays alone at every opportunity.

Targets & criteria for success:
1. Dominic will wait quietly for his turn to speak during group activities of three minutes, initially for two mornings per week, increasing to five mornings per week.
2. Dominic will play with one other child, initially for two minutes, three days per week, rising to five minutes five days per week. (Plans to increase group size when this target has been achieved.)
Targets to be reached by: 1) 19.12.07. 2)19.12.07.

Strategies to be used:
1. Dominic can put a sticker on his achievement chart each time he waits quietly during group activities. Five stickers will mean he can play with the jigsaws for an extra session.
2. Dominic will be allowed an extra five minutes with the toy trains each time he achieves his target for structured activities.

Adults involved: *Mrs Davies (Early Years teacher) will work with Dominic in nursery. Dominic's Mum will use the IEP at home.*
Resources/equipment: *Activities as appropriate; Dominic's achievement chart and stickers; IEP for home.*

Date of next review: *19.12.07.*
Parent's/carer's comment: *I'll ensure Dominic's IEP is carried out at home. I'll work with Mrs Davies too.*

Practitioners' signatures: *Alyson Davies (Early Years teacher); Claire Fredericks (SENCO).*

How can I help the child manage his behaviour?

Sometimes the behaviour of a child with autism can be extremely disruptive and upsetting, but you have to help him to manage how he reacts to things. It is not easy and it may take a while, but the child can't do it on his own, so it is important that you work to reduce his unwanted behaviour and help him develop a more acceptable way of reacting to life's pressures.

Here are some suggestions for strategies you can try:

- recognise what leads to any unwanted behaviour and try to remove the child from the situation for a little while;
- find out what triggers his distress and try to sort it out;
- if you can't sort out the causes of the child's difficulties, find out about positive behaviour techniques that you can try. The SENCO or the local authority (LA) will be able to tell you where to go for help;
- try distracting the child's attention or giving him something relaxing to do or playing some soothing music;
- always be patient and positive; try not to get wound up by his behaviour;
- if you can, let him know it is his behaviour that is unacceptable, not him. Show him you love him;
- always give him plenty of praise for positive behaviour;
- set a clear limit for his behaviour and stick to it. Make sure everybody else in the setting sticks to the rules too;
- make sure you always react to his unwanted behaviour in the same way every time, for example, don't chastise him for something today and then completely ignore the same behaviour tomorrow;
- any sanction has to be meaningful to the child, so make sure you choose carefully, for example, if he loves playing with jigsaws, making him do without jigsaws will mean more than other things you deprive him of;
- make sure the child has his sanction immediately. He will not be able to connect a sanction you give later to what he did earlier;
- try to use positive language – tell him what you would like him to do, rather than what you don't want him to do, for example, *Charlie, come and look at this book* rather than *Charlie, don't wander around the room* or *That was a really good try, Waseem – now let's have a go at it like this* rather than *Oh, you didn't manage it – never mind*;
- avoid letting the child indulge in ritualistic behaviours all the time, since this may prevent him from learning new skills and concepts. You can use the ritual or obsession as a starting point for introducing new skills but then try to wean him off it;

In the setting itself, there is plenty you can do to help the child feel comfortable and settled. Here are some strategies to try:

- make sure you face the child when speaking. He needs to see your face while you are speaking so he can glean as much information as he can about what you are saying, from the other clues such as the non-verbal gestures, facial expression and so on. But – be sensitive to the child who finds this distressing. Do not assume that the child who does not make or maintain eye contact is not listening to you – he may find it easier to concentrate on what you are saying when looking away from you;
- make sure your facial expression is always relaxed and warm. Sometimes this is the main way children have to read your feelings and attitude, so make it positive and welcoming;
- attract the child's attention by gently touching his shoulder and saying his name before giving instructions or information. This catching of his attention before you speak is crucial. Do it whatever the working situation, but – make sure the child is comfortable with this; do not touch him if that is something he really does not like;
- do not turn away your face until you have finished speaking. It is easy to do this without realising it, but if you turn away with only half a sentence spoken towards the child, he may miss the rest of your message;
- give instructions in small 'bite size' amounts, if necessary one element at a time. Children may retain only the first or the last part of an instruction and become extremely confused about what they were supposed to do, so give only as much instruction as the child can handle at one time;
- watch for any personality clashes – change the routine to avoid difficult situations, if necessary. Child-practitioner clashes can happen as well as child-child clashes. If it is happening in your setting, plan the day's activities to make sure people who do not get on with each other do not work together because neither the child nor the practitioner will be happy, and it is certain that effective learning will not happen.

Case study

Edward has Asperger's syndrome and is in Reception class, with one teacher (Mary B.) and one learning support assistant (Sue J.). Sue has not worked before with a child who has an ASD and finds it difficult to empathise with Edward's difficulties. She considers him a 'strange' child and is convinced that he is just an attention-seeker. Two mothers of other children in Edward's class are Sue's friends. She has discovered through talking with them outside school that some of the carers are not happy at Edward's presence in the class. They feel he is taking up time and attention that should be given to the other children who are more deserving, and they also feel he is lowering the standards. This makes Sue feel even more negative towards the child. Edward and Sue seem to be on a collision course.

- *discover the child's preferred learning style and stick to it. Observe the child and see whether his style is visual, auditory or kinaesthetic, or a combination of these. Plan the work and use appropriate resources to optimise the child's style. Does the child have monotropic attention, ie. can he concentrate on only one thing at a time, and is he easily distracted? If so, allow for this: give him a few moments to get back on track, give him some re-focusing time before you move on. What about groupings: does he prefer 1:1, small groups, large groups? Gradually change the learning situation to include all types. Does the child learn better with a computer? Does he need lots of concrete examples? Does he prefer to learn through books?*
- *learn to use equipment, communication systems or other special facilities that the child may have. For example, this could be Picture Exchange System or Makaton signing. Learning the child's method of communication is well worth the effort!*
- *have a timeline or pictorial timetable on display for the day's activities. Make sure it is displayed at child-eye height, and give the child a set of cards that duplicate the symbols on the timeline. Warn the child in advance of changes of activity with, for example, an egg timer or alarm clock. When the sand drops to the bottom of the glass, Simon, it will be time to put away the jigsaw and go into the hall.*
- *keep to the daily routine as much as possible. This ensures security and stability, which is essential, especially for children with ASDs.*
- *keep furniture and designated areas in the same place and keep the layout of apparatus the same. Children with ASDs particularly need the security of knowing where things are and will be when they want to use them again.*
- *have a quiet area always available. The children benefit from having somewhere they can go to get their heads together, particularly after a confrontation or a misunderstanding. It must never be used as a sin-bin; it must be a pleasurable place to go! Try putting a CD player in there with CDs of soothing music. Mozart works particularly well for children with ASDs.*
- *have a 'bland' and non-stimulating work area for the child who is overwhelmed with 'busy' displays or bright colours. Sometimes the child feels totally swamped by what's going on around him. The natural 'busyness' of early years settings can trigger serious distress in a child with ASD, simply because he can't handle the sensory overload. A bland corner (grey paper on the wall, no displays) can often help.*
- *use dolls, puppets and visual aids as part of story time, circle time or group discussions. This supports the child and helps him to make sense of what's going on – it gives a solidity to the abstraction of language. Some children can communicate better through a persona doll or puppet.*
- *make labels and cards with tactile materials. Use sandpaper, fabrics with a deep nap such as velvet, bubble wrap, or corrugated paper. Some children with ASD are very tactile and can learn well through kinaesthetic approaches.*

Pause for thought

Think back to the case study above with Edward and Sue. In what ways can this situation be resolved? Look at it from the points of view of Sue, the other parents, the class teacher and Edward, and see what suggestions you can make. Why does the situation appear to be breaking down? What can the class teacher do? What should Sue do? Or, indeed, not do?

Discuss this with a colleague and see what strategies you both come up with. This is a useful exercise to do, as the time may come when you have to tackle another member of staff in your setting for their less-than-helpful approach to a child with ASD.

How can the setting support the child's carers?

What you can do to help the child's carers will probably depend on their emotional and psychological stage. If the child has only recently been diagnosed as having ASD, the carers may need some help themselves before they (and therefore you) can help the child.

If they have known about the child's difficulties for a while, though, and they feel stronger about the whole thing, they may be ready to get stuck in and work with you on planning the best way forward for ensuring the child's entitlements.

Case study

Matthew, aged four, was diagnosed with ASD at two and a half years old. He went to nursery in the mornings where his behaviour caused problems for everybody. He had severe temper tantrums, screaming and throwing toys across the room. He didn't say very much to the adults, but he would nod or shake his head, and he never spoke to or played with the other children. He loved jigsaws and always did them in exactly the same way each time. The staff asked Matthew's Mum to help them with managing his behaviour.

She told them that dressing and undressing, and lots of bright colours upset him. The teachers realised that Matthew's tantrums usually happened just at playtime or PE sessions, when he had to stop his game and put on his coat, or an apron for cooking or painting. They also realised the bright displays and posters in the nursery affected him.

They made a small area in the working room very bland by putting a soft-green paper on the wall, and they worked with Matthew in this space. They put a timetable on the wall with pictures showing the activities, and helped Matthew to keep a check on when it was activity changeover time. He had an alarm clock for this, and he was able to manage himself without the same distress. Eventually he dealt with dressing and undressing and even changes in his activities in a much calmer way.

Matthew's experience is fairly common and you may recognise parts of it. Because Matthew's Mum and practitioners worked together and shared their knowledge of Matthew, they were able to plan ways of helping him to make sense of what was going on around him.

What if the carers need support from the setting?

It is important that the carers feel confident in working with you as the child's practitioner. If they have additional needs themselves, you should take this into account and make arrangements to ensure they are involved. If they have learning difficulties or they use an alternative communication system, for example, you should approach this sensitively and make sure the carers are completely comfortable.

Problems caused by ASDs are classed as special educational needs, and so the carers and the child have the right to any support and help offered by the LA. You must make sure you give the carers the contact details of the local Parent Partnership Service (PPS).

If English is not the carers' first language and they would like some support from somebody within their community with translation and even moral support,

they have the right to ask for this. If you arrange for an interpreter for the carers during meetings, make sure he is good. Sometimes misunderstandings can happen because of a poor translation.

If the carers have disabilities or difficulties and they would like help in working with you, assure them they need only ask. If they have had a bad personal experience of SEN education themselves, they may be feeling uneasy. Hopefully times have changed and settings are much more sensitive and supportive. Reassure the carers that you will keep this in mind when you are planning together.

When you have all planned a Play plan or an IEP, you will probably ask the carers to do some activities with the child at home. Here are some tips to pass on to them for Happy Home-Sessions.

• if they are not sure how to do the activity, tell them

to ask you to explain again or even demonstrate – it is important to get it right!
- ask them to stop doing the activity as soon as the child gets bored, distracted or distressed. They can try again later;
- advise them to time the sessions well – not just before the child's favourite TV programme, or when he wants his dinner;

- if they think the activity is not helping the child to achieve his target, ask them to mention this to you and you can change it;
- ask them to stop the activity when the child's on a winning streak, and always end the session by praising his efforts. You want him to be keen to do the next session, so get the carers to make it fun and successful.

What advice can I give the carers themselves?

The child's carers and the rest of the family should not be making everything and everybody revolve around the child with ASD. Here are a few tips you can pass on to them. Choose your time wisely when you speak to them; and also speak to them with sensitivity.

Suggest they

- avoid overprotecting the child: the child must learn to become as independent as possible; carers can do harm by wrapping him in cotton wool;
- avoid isolating themselves and/or the family: social situations are not easy with a child who has ASD, and it is tempting for carers to stay at home, not accept or send out invitations, or have their groceries delivered; but becoming a hermit will not achieve anything, and may cause more harm than they realise;
- teach the child how to wait his turn: waiting is a fundamental part of daily living and he must learn this; give him a signal, a picture to hold or a sign when he has to wait – start off small, maybe five seconds or so, and gradually increase the time, until he is able to wait for however long he has to.

These tips may seem to be common sense and a small amount to ask, but carers will find that they are important points to take on board, and may take longer than they realise to achieve.

Is there anything else we could suggest the carers try at home?

The child is unique and so is the way he reacts to different things. There is no magic formula for helping him to overcome his symptoms, but there are some tried and true techniques that work with lots of children who have ASD. Here are a few of them – if one doesn't work, ask the carers to try another.

Suggest they

- put up some pictures or a chart that show their child's daily routines: for example, on their bedroom wall put up pictures of the stages of getting up, including the order of putting on their clothes (they can use pictures from catalogues and magazines – if the child is ready they can put words and labels on the pictures too); on the kitchen wall they could have a chart showing breakfast, leaving for school and arriving at school; by seeing exactly what happens next in his day, the child will be more reassured and less confused about the world around him;
- pinpoint anything in the house or their routine that triggers anxiety or unwanted behaviour in the child: change it if they can; if they can't change it, then try to find ways of helping the child to tolerate it without becoming anxious or distressed;
- try speaking to the child using his name first: if the child doesn't mind physical contact, gently touch him on the arm as they say the child's name;
- always work in small steps in a logical way when they are doing an activity together: if what they are doing seems too difficult then they should make the size of the steps smaller; for example, if they are showing the child how to fasten his buttons and he just doesn't get it, suggest the carer fastens all the buttons except the last one, and then encourages the child to do that one; next time, do all the buttons except the last two, and so on, until

gradually the child is fastening most or all of the buttons;
- give instructions one at a time: if possible they could have some pictures showing the steps of the job and talk about these before they get the child to do the job itself;
- use the child's interests, skills and/or their favourite routine as a starting point for something new he has to learn or understand: new ideas mean change to a child with ASD, and change is what he dislikes most; by using his interests, the carers can introduce new skills or ideas and then gradually move on to using other ways of practising the new skill;
- use activities that the child enjoys in his language-based activities: this will help to encourage him to speak with, play with or generally share with other people, especially his brothers, sisters and friends.

- teach a language skill in a situation or in a concrete way that is familiar to the child: trying to teach a skill in an abstract or airy-fairy way will not work; for example, if they are trying to help him to understand things like under, through, on top, over. Suggest they make a game of it by getting the child to put small toys in different places, using the words they are teaching: 'Hide the car under the cushion' or 'Put the toy on top of the television' and so on.
- always give the child lots of praise and encouragement: even if his attempts are not getting him very far at first, especially with language-based activities; because language can be very hard for a child with ASD, he needs to feel confident in using it; knocking him back with constant correction or criticism will only put him off.

How do we review IEPs with the carers?

Play plans are not quite as formal as IEPs and so would not need to have an 'official' review. This doesn't mean, however, that they are not an important part of your strategy to support the child. Quite the opposite, and, as such, they should be regularly monitored and reviewed with the carers, on an informal level.

IEPs, on the other hand, are programmes planned with the SEN Code of Practice guidelines at their root, so are regarded as more formal documents, requiring formal reviews. They should be officially reviewed at least once per term and, in the case of very young children, more often, as a review can be called at any time.

Here are a few tips for holding a successful review

- arrange for an interpreter if English is not the carers' first language;
- make the room cheerful and welcoming, with coffee and biscuits and some flowers;
- give the carers a chance to relax by inviting them a few minutes before the official start time;
- some carers feel threatened or intimidated by the review, so don't organise the room as if for a formal interview: put the chairs in a circle, with a low table in the middle;
- help to keep everybody focused on each point as it comes up for discussion by working your way through the Review Form systematically;
- make sure the key worker offers a contribution; this is crucial, as he knows the child most intimately within the setting;
- design a Carer's Review Form and give it to the carers some time before the review. It will help them to focus on what they would like to say in the meeting. Make sure that the carers and the child, if appropriate, can offer their input to the meeting;

- If the child is able to make a contribution to the discussion but not at the meeting, he can do this through the carers on a Child's Review Form or by adding his comments to the Carer's Review Form. Encourage the carers to record on it what the child says or thinks about the IEP, and his progress. Talk the form(s) through with the carers beforehand and make sure they are happy about completing it;
- as Chair, you can bring the focus back to the discussion and give the other people present a chance to have their say. Ensure that everybody has time to speak, but don't let people hog the limelight;

- on the review form, you can record the plan of further action as a simple Yes/No deletion, for simplicity's sake. The details will go on a new IEP form;
- at the end, clear up any misunderstandings immediately by briefly summarising what was said, asking whether everybody agrees. Ask them all to initial your notes before they leave;
- book the date of the next review immediately;
- sign and date the Review Form. If possible, give the carers a copy immediately;
- make sure the carers are happy with the review's outcome: have a quiet word with them afterwards. Make sure you do this sensitively and in a supportive way. This is especially important for carers who are diffident, or who feel upset or threatened. If they need to have the paperwork explained to them, talk it through with them in a way that is respectful, yet enables them to understand;
- send copies of the Review Form to everybody who attended the meeting as soon as possible so that any queries can be clarified more or less straight away. Also send a copy to relevant people who did not attend;

You must monitor the child and the IEP between reviews in case the programme is not working. If you think you have done some poor planning, it is crucial that you act immediately. Call an interim review to discuss your concerns with carers and other staff involved, and then change the IEP.

Pause for thought

You are chairing a review on an IEP for Freddie, who has Asperger's syndrome. He is working with you, a Learning Support Assistant and his Mum. The LA's educational psychologist is also involved but sees Freddie about once per term (usually shortly before a review), when she comes into the setting to conduct some tests.

At the review, one of the professionals tends to dominate the discussions, pushing forward his theories about 'what's wrong' with Freddie, and what programme he should be following. He also uses a great many acronyms, which causes confusion for Freddie's Mum, who clearly has no idea of what the professional is talking about. How, as Chair, would you handle this situation?

You could discuss this with a colleague as a 'share-session'.

How does the setting work with other professionals?

It depends very much on your LA which other professionals you might work with in supporting a child with ASD. The age of the child will also be a deciding factor, as will the family's situation regarding the involvement of other professionals, such as the Health Visitor or a social worker.

On a day-to-day basis you will, of course, be working with your colleagues in the setting. They will be involved in helping to plan the child's programmes, but also the setting's special educational needs (SEN) policy. Let's have a closer look at some of the other professionals you may be involved with in the table below.

Early years support teacher or adviser

Your LA is likely to have a specialist early years teacher or adviser who will visit your setting and offer advice and help on all aspects of working with a child who has ASD. If ASD is not his exact specialist field, he will be able to refer you to the person within the LA who is best placed to answer your questions.

Educational psychologist

Every LA has educational psychologists attached to it, and their job is to work with a child, his family and the educational practitioners to tackle the child's problems. They can check what achievement level the child has, and then make good practical suggestions for ways that you and the carers can work together to help the child.

Speech and language therapist (SLT)

The child may be referred to a speech and language therapist who will test his speech and language skills in order to see how he has developed. He may see the child in a clinic or he may come into the setting – this depends on the system where you work. How often he will see the child after the first meeting or two will depend on a few things; for example, what the problem is, how severe it is, what the plan of action is to help and support the child. You will almost certainly be invited to be involved in the plan of action by doing educational activities and games in the setting. You may be able to borrow some of the equipment that the SLT uses in his sessions with the child.

Educational welfare officer (EWO)

EWOs are attached to the education department of your LA and usually they have social work training. Their job is to work with children, carers, settings and schools to find the best solution to problems that are affecting the child. Some children with ASDs develop emotional and behavioural problems which affect their schoolwork, and the EWO may be able to help. Although unlikely at the early years stage, you may be involved with an EWO.

Family doctor (GP or General Practitioner)

The family's GP will be involved when the child is diagnosed as having ASD and you may or may not be working with him. The doctor might refer the child and carers to:

- the health visitor
- a counsellor
- the child mental health service
- the adult mental health service
- the social services

Social worker

Social workers become actively involved with the child's family if the carers ask for input, or if the family's difficulties are very worrying. Again, you may or may not be closely involved, depending on the situation.

Child psychotherapist or child psychiatrist (CP)

If the child also has behavioural or emotional problems that are very worrying, he may be referred to a CP, who will discuss the child's problems with the carers (and possibly ask for your contribution), check the child's achievement level and then plan a programme of action. This can include many ways of helping, such as:

- family therapy
- music therapy
- play therapy
- art therapy
- counselling
- behaviour therapy
- psychological support.

The inclusive SEN policy

Working with other professionals also entails writing an inclusive SEN policy together which you will all implement in the setting. This policy, by definition, will address the needs of children with ASD.

In this section, we will explore the rationale behind writing an SEN policy and look at some issues which should answer your questions about 'how it is done'.

Let's start by discussing

- what a policy is, why it should be written and what it should include;
- how adults involved with the setting should examine their own attitudes, beliefs and practices as part of the policy-planning process;
- how planning the policy should include everybody involved with the setting, especially the children and their carers;
- who puts the policy into practice.

What is a policy?

All early years settings which receive government funding must write and put into practice an SEN policy. Apart from this compulsory requirement, it is an opportunity for you all to review your practices and philosophy, and to focus on inclusion.

For this reason, private and non-maintained settings should also consider writing and implementing their own policies.

A policy is a working document produced by people involved with your setting and stating what your aims are with regard to the children in your care. A bit of hard work in the early stages of planning will mean effective practice when the policy is implemented. Well-planned and carefully thought-through policies are invaluable to practitioners, because they provide guidelines for good practice.

Why should your setting plan an SEN policy?

All early years settings have the care of some children with SEN in general, and some with ASD in particular. Many practitioners have not specialised in SEN (or indeed in ASDs) and find it helpful to refer to an SEN policy as a basic guide for what is expected within their setting. The following reasons show why having an SEN policy is good practice:

- it offers support, help and encouragement to everybody in the setting, particularly if they feel unsure about how to work with a child who has ASD;

- it helps to ensure the smooth running of the setting, providing it is put into practice by everybody involved;
- it helps to ensure that everybody involved in the setting is respected and valued, as are their opinions;
- it encourages caring, inclusive attitudes by everybody towards each other;
- it fosters a positive and constructive atmosphere within the setting;
- it recognises and acknowledges everybody's place in, and commitment to, inclusive practices in the setting;

What needs to be written into an SEN policy?

The SEN Code of Practice suggests what you should include in your SEN policy. Among the most important are the following:

- information about the setting's provisions, including the aims and objectives of the policy. What are your aims in the policy you are drawing up? Are you aiming for inclusion of children with ASDs? Does your policy make sure that happens?
- the name of the SENCO and any specialities offered by members of staff. If a practitioner within your setting has a qualification or training in the field of ASDs, they should be named in the policy together with what their speciality is. For example, 'Our SENCO, Laura Smith, has a B.Phil.Ed. and has specialised in working with children who have autistic spectrum disorders';
- the criteria for evaluating the success of the SEN policy. When and how will the policy be reviewed? How will everybody decide its strengths and weaknesses? How will you make any required changes? Because it is used on a daily basis, the policy's weaknesses will soon become apparent. You should check how serious these are and how quickly they need to be addressed. There isn't a blueprint because each setting is unique;
- the arrangements for provision for children who have ASDs. How are you going to

support children with ASDs with regard to resources, staffing, time and so on? Have a look at the way the setting is organised, run, staffed and equipped. Review these and make sure each element includes children with ASDs, adapting them if necessary;

- the arrangements for admission of children with ASDs. You will need to agree your setting's approach to how children with ASDs are admitted. For example, will you have a transition or familiarisation period? Will you invite carers to stay with the child initially?
- the arrangements for identifying and assessing SEN/ASDs . Who does your identification and assessments? When, where and how? Is it done at a set time, or at a time when the assessor happens to be 'free' to do it? Will it be done either in the setting's usual daily activity sessions or during a special assessment/observation session? Will it be done by the child's own practitioner, the SENCO or your setting's head/manager? What form will the assessments take? What will be used? For example, the Foundation stage profile, standardised assessments, and the type of observation;
- the arrangements for providing support for children with ASDs. Review your resources and how you use them. Can the equipment, games and activities be effectively and appropriately used by children with ASDs? For example, if Freddie hates role play and usually has a 'fly-off' when he is asked to do it, while you are supporting him in controlling his ASD, give him something else to do; if his IEP says his reward is an extra session on the computer, make sure you have enough computers in the room;
- the arrangements for providing access by the child with ASDs to a balanced and broadly based curriculum. How will you make sure that the child

with ASD has the opportunities and experiences of the full curriculum on offer, whether this is the Foundation stage or the National Curriculum? Do you need to adjust the timetable, the venue, the staffing, the resources or equipment to ensure that everything that is on offer to all the children is also on offer to the children with ASDs? Review how you plan and implement Play plans or IEPs, making sure that your procedures do actually result in effective support for each child;
- the procedures for reviewing the needs of a child with ASDs. When, where and how will reviews of each child's progress be carried out? Who will be involved? While the guidance in the SEN Code of Practice offers suggestions, some things are unique to each setting. You need to consider your facilities, timetable, staffing and clientele, in the decision-making.

Do you need copies of the policy translated into other languages? If you do, make sure that the translation is of a high standard and accurate.

Who puts the policy into practice?

Let's have a look at some roles and responsibilities:

- the planning, writing, publishing and reviewing of the policy must be done by everybody appropriately involved with the setting;
- the management of the policy is the manager or head's responsibility;
- the day-to-day operation of the policy is the Special Educational Needs Coordinator's (SENCO) task;

- the implementation of the policy is done by all other involved adults within their own area;

The strengths and weaknesses of the policy will be highlighted through the day-to-day practicalities of using it.

Case study

Mrs Davies enrolled her son, Adam, at his local primary school, to begin the Reception class in September. Adam was diagnosed with Asperger's syndrome when he was three and a half, and attended a private nursery for five mornings per week.

The Headteacher of the school gave Mrs Davies a copy of the SEN policy, and she was delighted to read that the SENCO had attended several in-service courses dealing with ASDs. The policy also outlined the school's procedures for working closely with parents in the planning and review of IEPs.

Mrs Davies gave the Headteacher copies of Adam's records from the nursery, which ensured that the school staff would put a smooth and seamless transition action plan into place. Adam started the term gradually, attending part-time for the first couple of weeks, attending full-time just after his fifth birthday in the middle of September.

Mrs Davies said 'The SEN policy has helped me to see who does what at the school. Even though the SENCO isn't Adam's teacher, she works closely with all of us and we have written an IEP that Adam is working to. We will be reviewing it at Christmas. I am not worried now, as the policy also explains exactly what will happen at the review.'

Pause for thought

Think of one child you have worked with in the past, who puzzled you, perhaps because some of his behavioural traits were similar to those we have just looked at.

What was it about the child that made you wonder how he ticked? Did you share your thoughts with anybody in the setting? Did you speak to the child's carers about your feelings? How did you work with the child in the end? Looking back, do you feel your planning for the child was appropriate? Did it help the child to achieve and develop? If the answer is Yes, could or would you have done anything more and/or differently? If No, what would you change about the approach you took?

Well, do you think differently now?

Useful Contacts

The National Autistic Society
393 City Road, London EC1V 1NG. UK
Tel: 020 7833 2299. Fax: 020 7833 9666
Email: nas@nas.org.uk. www.nas.org.uk
(The Society has contact details of local autistic societies as well as a treasure trove of other useful information and advice.)

The Scottish Society for Autism
Hilton House, Alloa Business Park, The Whins, Alloa, FK10 3SA
Phone: 01259 720044. Fax: 01259 720051
E-mail: info@autism-in-scotland.org.uk www.autism-in-scotland.org.uk

Autism Cymru
6 Great Darkgate Street. Aberystwyth, Ceredigion, SY23 1DE
Phone: 01970 625256. Fax: 01970 639454
www.autismcymru.org.uk

Autism Northern Ireland
Donard House, Knockbracken Healthcare Park, Saintfield Road, Belfast, BT8 8BH
Phone: Helpline Mon/Wed/Fri 9.30-1pm 0845 055 9010, Switchboard 028 90 401729 Fax: 028 90 403467
Email: info@autism.orh www.autismni.org

Autism Research Unit
School of Health, Natural & Social Sciences, City Campus, University of Sunderland, Sunderland, SR1 3SD
Tel: 0191 510 8922. Fax: 0191 567 0420
Email: autism.unit@sunderland.ac.uk www.osiris.sunderland.ac.uk/autism/

Contact a Family
209 – 211 City Road, London, EC1V 1JN
Tel: 020 7608 8700. Fax: 020 7608 8701 Free Helpline: 0808 808 3555
Email: info@cafamily.org.uk. www.cafamily.org.uk

Network 81
1 – 7 Woodfield Terrace, Stansted, Essex, CM24 8AJ
Helpline: 0870 770 3306. Admin: 0870 770 3262 Fax: 0870 770 3263
Email: info@network81.org www.network81.org
(This is a national network of carers working towards properly resourced inclusive education for children with special needs.)

The Children's Legal Centre
University of Essex, Wivenhoe Park, Colchester, Essex, CO4 3SQ
Tel: 01206 872 466. Fax: 01206 874 026
Education Law Advice Line: 0845 456 6811
Email: clc@essex.ac.uk www.childrenslegalcentre.com

British Institute of Learning Disabilities
Campion House, Green Street, Kidderminster, Worcestershire, DY10 1JL
Tel: 01562 723010. Fax: 01562 723029
Email: enquiries@bild.org.uk www.bild.org.uk

All these websites were accessed and contact details checked in July 2007.